RUBÁIYÁT OF OMAR KHAYYÁM

RUBÁIYÁT OF
OMAR KHAYYÁM

THE ASTRONOMER-POET OF PERSIA

Rendered into English Verse by
EDWARD FITZGERALD

Edited by
W. ALDIS WRIGHT

MACMILLAN
LONDON · MELBOURNE · TORONTO
ST MARTIN'S PRESS. NEW YORK
1967

MACMILLAN AND COMPANY LIMITED
Little Essex Street London WC 2
also Bombay Calcutta Madras Melbourne

ST MARTIN'S PRESS INC
175 Fifth Avenue New York NY 10010

SBN 333 01611 4

Reprinted 1973

PRINTED IN GREAT BRITAIN

CONTENTS

OMAR KHAYYÁM

THE

ASTRONOMER-POET OF PERSIA

OMAR KHAYYÁM was born at Naishápúr in Khorassán in the latter half of our Eleventh, and died within the First Quarter of our Twelfth Century. The slender Story of his Life is curiously twined about that of two other very considerable Figures in their Time and Country: one of whom tells the Story of all Three. This was Nizám ul Mulk, Vizyr to Alp Arslán the Son, and Malik Shah the Grandson, of Toghrul Beg the Tartar, who had wrested Persia from the feeble Successor of Mahmúd the Great, and founded that Seljukian Dynasty which

E

finally roused Europe into the Crusades.   This
Nizám ul Mulk, in his *Wasiyat*—or *Testament*—
which he wrote and left as a Memorial for future
Statesmen—relates the following, as quoted in the
Calcutta Review, No. lix., from Mirkhond's *History
of the Assassins.*

"'One of the greatest of the wise men of
Khorassán was the Imám Mowaffak of Naishápúr,
a man highly honoured and reverenced—may God
rejoice his soul; his illustrious years exceeded
eighty-five, and it was the universal belief that
every boy who read the Koran or studied the
traditions in his presence, would assuredly attain to
honour and happiness.   For this cause did my father
send me from Tús to Naishápúr with Abd-us-samad,
the doctor of law, that I might employ myself in
study and learning under the guidance of that
illustrious teacher.   Towards me he ever turned an
eye of favour and kindness, and as his pupil I felt
for him extreme affection and devotion, so that I

passed four years in his service. When I first came there, I found two other pupils of mine own age newly arrived, Hakim Omar Khayyám, and the ill-fated Ben Sabbáh. Both were endowed with sharpness of wit and the highest natural powers ; and we three formed a close friendship together. When the Imám rose from his lectures, they used to join me, and we repeated to each other the lessons we had heard. Now Omar was a native of Naishápúr, while Hasan Ben Sabbáh's father was one Ali, a man of austere life and practice, but heretical in his creed and doctrine. One day Hasan said to me and to Khayyám, " It is a universal belief that the pupils of the Imám Mowaffak will attain to fortune. Now, even if we *all* do not attain thereto, without doubt one of us will ; what then shall be our mutual pledge and bond ? " We answered, " Be it what you please." —" Well, " he said, " let us make a vow, that to whomsoever this fortune falls, he shall share it equally with the rest, and reserve no pre-eminence for himself. "—" Be it so, " we both replied, and on those terms we mutually pledged our words.   Years rolled on, and I went from Khorassán to Transoxiana, and wandered to Ghazni and Cabul ; and when I returned, I was invested with office, and rose to be administrator of affairs during the Sultanate of Sultan Alp Arslán.'

"He goes on to state, that years passed by, and both his old school-friends found him out, and came and claimed a share in his good fortune, according to the school-day vow.   The Vizier was generous and kept his word.   Hasan demanded a place in the government, which the Sultan granted at the Vizier's request ; but, discontented with a gradual rise, he plunged into the maze of intrigue of an Oriental Court, and, failing in a base attempt to supplant his benefactor, he was disgraced and fell.   After many mishaps and wanderings, Hasan became the head of the Persian sect of the *Ismaílians*,—a party of fanatics who had long murmured in obscurity, but rose to an evil eminence under the guidance of his strong and evil will. In A.D. 1090, he seized the castle of Alamút, in the province of Rúdbar, which lies in the mountainous tract south of the Caspian Sea ; and it was from this mountain home he obtained that evil celebrity among the Crusaders as the OLD MAN OF THE MOUN-TAINS, and spread terror through the Mohammedan world ; and it is yet disputed whether the word *Assassin*, which they have left in the language of modern Europe as their dark memorial, is derived from the *hashish*, or opiate of hemp-leaves (the Indian *bhang*), with which they maddened themselves to the sullen pitch of Oriental desperation, or from the name of the founder of the dynasty, whom we have seen in his quiet collegiate days, at Naishápúr. One of the countless victims of the Assassin's dagger was Nizám ul Mulk himself, the old school-boy friend.[1]

[1] Some of Omar's Rubáiyát warn us of the danger of Greatness, the instability of Fortune, and while advocating Charity to all Men, recommending us to be too intimate with none. Attár makes Nizám ul Mulk use the very words of his

"Omar Khayyám also came to the Vizier to claim his share ; but not to ask for title or office. 'The greatest boon you can confer on me,' he said, 'is to let me live in a corner under the shadow of your fortune, to spread wide the advantages of Science, and pray for your long life and prosperity.' The Vizier tells us, that, when he found Omar was really sincere in his refusal, he pressed him no further, but granted him a yearly pension of 1200 *mithkáls* of gold, from the treasury of Naishápúr.

"At Naishápúr thus lived and died Omar Khayyám, 'busied,' adds the Vizier, 'in winning knowledge of every kind, and especially in Astronomy, wherein he attained to a very high pre-eminence. Under the Sultanate of Malik Shah, he came to Merv, and obtained great praise for his proficiency in science, and the Sultan showered favours upon him.'

friend Omar [Rub. xxviii.], " When Nizám ul Mulk was in the Agony (of Death) he said, 'Oh God ! I am passing away in the hand of the Wind.' "

"When Malik Shah determined to reform the calendar, Omar was one of the eight learned men employed to do it; the result was the *Jaláli* era (so called from *Jalál-ud-din*, one of the king's names)— 'a computation of time,' says Gibbon, 'which surpasses the Julian, and approaches the accuracy of the Gregorian style.' He is also the author of some astronomical tables, entitled Zíji-Maliksháhí," and the French have lately republished and translated an Arabic Treatise of his on Algebra.

"His Takhallus or poetical name (Khayyám) signifies a Tentmaker, and he is said to have at one time exercised that trade, perhaps before Nizám ul Mulk's generosity raised him to independence. Many Persian poets similarly derive their names from their occupations; thus we have Attár, 'a druggist,' Assár, 'an oil presser,' etc.[1] Omar

---

[1] Though all these, like our Smiths, Archers, Millers, Fletchers, etc., may simply retain the Surname of an hereditary calling.

himself alludes to his name in the following whimsical
lines :—

> " ' Khayyám, who stitched the tents of science,
>   Has fallen in grief's furnace and been suddenly burned ;
>   The shears of Fate have cut the tent ropes of his life,
>   And the broker of Hope has sold him for nothing ! '

"We have only one more anecdote to give of his
Life, and that relates to the close ; it is told in the
anonymous preface which is sometimes prefixed to
his poems ; it has been printed in the Persian in the
Appendix to Hyde's *Veterum Persarum Religio*, p.
499 ; and D'Herbelot alludes to it in his Bibliothèque, under *Khiam :* [1]—

" ' It is written in the chronicles of the ancients
that this King of the Wise, Omar Khayyám, died at
Naishápúr in the year of the Hegira 517 (A.D.
1123) ; in science he was unrivalled,—the very

---

[1] " Philosophe Musulman qui a vêcu en Odeur de Sainteté
dans sa Religion, vers la Fin du premier et le Commencement
du second Siècle," no part of which, except the " Philosophe,"
can apply to our Khayyám.

paragon of his age. Khwájah Nizámi of Samarcand,
who was one of his pupils, relates the following story:
" I often used to hold conversations with my teacher
Omar Khayyám, in a garden ; and one day he said
to me, ' My tomb shall be in a spot where the north
wind may scatter roses over it.' I wondered at the
words he spake, but I knew that his were no idle
words.[1] Years after, when I chanced to revisit

---

[1] The Rashness of the Words, according to D'Herbelot,
consisted in being so opposed to those in the Korán : " No
Man knows where he shall die."—This story of Omar reminds
me of another so naturally—and when one remembers how
wide of his humble mark the noble sailor aimed—so pathetically
told by Captain Cook—not by Doctor Hawkesworth—in his
Second Voyage (i. 374). When leaving Ulietea, " Oreo's last
request was for me to return. When he saw he could not
obtain that promise, he asked the name of my *Marai* (burying-
place). As strange a question as this was, I hesitated not a
moment to tell him ' Stepney' ; the parish in which I live when
in London. I was made to repeat it several times over till
they could pronounce it ; and then 'Stepney Marai no Toote'
was echoed through an hundred mouths at once. I afterwards
found the same question had been put to Mr. Forster by a man
on shore ; but he gave a different, and indeed more proper

Naishápúr, I went to his final resting-place, and lo!
it was just outside a garden, and trees laden with
fruit stretched their boughs over the garden wall,
and dropped their flowers upon his tomb, so that the
stone was hidden under them." ' "

Thus far—without fear of Trespass—from the
Calcutta Review.   The writer of it, on reading in
India this story of Omar's Grave, was reminded, he
says, of Cicero's Account of finding Archimedes'
Tomb at Syracuse, buried in grass and weeds.   I
think Thorwaldsen desired to have roses grow over
him ; a wish religiously fulfilled for him to the
present day, I believe.   However, to return to Omar.

Though the Sultan "shower'd Favours upon
him," Omar's Epicurean Audacity of Thought and
Speech caused him to be regarded askance in his
own Time and Country.   He is said to have been
especially hated and dreaded by the Súfis, whose

answer, by saying, ' No man who used the sea could say where
he should be buried.' "

Practice he ridiculed, and whose Faith amounts to little more than his own, when stript of the Mysticism and formal recognition of Islamism under which Omar would not hide. Their Poets, including Háfiz, who are (with the exception of Firdausi) the most considerable in Persia, borrowed largely, indeed, of Omar's material, but turning it to a mystical Use more convenient to Themselves and the People they addressed; a People quite as quick of Doubt as of Belief; as keen of Bodily Sense as of Intellectual; and delighting in a cloudy composition of both, in which they could float luxuriously between Heaven and Earth, and this World and the Next, on the wings of a poetical expression, that might serve indifferently for either. Omar was too honest of Heart as well as of Head for this. Having failed (however mistakenly) of finding any Providence but Destiny, and any World but This, he set about making the most of it; preferring rather to soothe the Soul through the Senses into Acquiescence with

Things as he saw them, than to perplex it with vain disquietude after what they *might* be. It has been seen, however, that his Worldly Ambition was not exorbitant ; and he very likely takes a humorous or perverse pleasure in exalting the gratification of Sense above that of the Intellect, in which he must have taken great delight, although it failed to answer the Questions in which he, in common with all men, was most vitally interested.

For whatever Reason, however, Omar, as before said, has never been popular in his own Country, and therefore has been but scantily transmitted abroad. The MSS. of his Poems, mutilated beyond the average Casualties of Oriental Transcription, are so rare in the East as scarce to have reacht Westward at all, in spite of all the acquisitions of Arms and Science. There is no copy at the India House, none at the Bibliothèque Nationale of Paris. We know but of one in England : No. 140 of the Ouseley MSS. at the Bodleian, written at Shiráz, A.D. 1460.

This contains but 158 Rubáiyát. One in the Asiatic Society's Library at Calcutta (of which we have a Copy) contains (and yet incomplete) 516, though swelled to that by all kinds of Repetition and Corruption. So Von Hammer speaks of *his* Copy as containing about 200, while Dr. Sprenger catalogues the Lucknow MS. at double that number.[1] The Scribes, too, of the Oxford and Calcutta MSS. seem to do their Work under a sort of Protest; each beginning with a Tetrastich (whether genuine or not), taken out of its alphabetical order; the Oxford with one of Apology; the Calcutta with one of Expostulation, supposed (says a Notice prefixed to the MS.) to have arisen from a Dream, in which Omar's mother asked about his future fate. It may be rendered thus—

> " Oh Thou who burn'st in Heart for those who burn
>   In Hell, whose fires thyself shall feed in turn ;
>   How long be crying, ' Mercy on them, God !'
>   Why, who art Thou to teach, and He to learn?"

---

1 " Since this Paper was written " (adds the Reviewer in a

The Bodleian Quatrain pleads Pantheism by way of Justification.

> " If I myself upon a looser Creed
>   Have loosely strung the Jewel of Good deed,
>   Let this one thing for my Atonement plead :
>   That One for Two I never did mis-read."

The Reviewer,[1] to whom I owe the Particulars of Omar's life, concludes his Review by comparing him with Lucretius, both as to natural Temper and Genius, and as acted upon by the Circumstances in which he lived.   Both indeed were men of subtle, strong, and cultivated Intellect, fine Imagination, and Hearts passionate for Truth and Justice ; who justly revolted from their Country's false Religion, and false, or foolish, Devotion to it ; but who fell short of replacing what they subverted by such better *Hope* as others, with no better Revelation to guide them,

note), "we have met with a Copy of a very rare Edition, printed at Calcutta in 1836.   This contains 438 Tetrastichs. with an Appendix containing 54 others not found in some MSS."

[1] Professor Cowell.

had yet made a Law to themselves. Lucretius, indeed, with such material as Epicurus furnished, satisfied himself with the theory of a vast machine fortuitously constructed, and acting by a Law that implied no Legislator; and so composing himself into a Stoical rather than Epicurean severity of Attitude, sat down to contemplate the mechanical Drama of the Universe which he was part Actor in; himself and all about him (as in his own sublime description of the Roman Theatre) discoloured with the lurid reflex of the Curtain suspended between the Spectator and the Sun. Omar, more desperate, or more careless of any so complicated System as resulted in nothing but hopeless Necessity, flung his own Genius and Learning with a bitter or humorous jest into the general Ruin which their insufficient glimpses only served to reveal; and, pretending sensual pleasure as the serious purpose of Life, only *diverted* himself with speculative problems of Deity, Destiny, Matter and Spirit, Good and Evil, and other

such questions, easier to start than to run down,
and the pursuit of which becomes a very weary
sport at last !

With regard to the present Translation. The
original Rubáiyát (as, missing an Arabic Guttural,
these *Tetrastichs* are more musically called) are
independent Stanzas, consisting each of four Lines of
equal, though varied, Prosody; sometimes *all* rhym-
ing, but oftener (as here imitated) the third line a
blank. Somewhat as in the Greek Alcaic, where the
penultimate line seems to lift and suspend the Wave
that falls over in the last. As usual with such kind
of Oriental Verse, the Rubáiyát follow one another
according to Alphabetic Rhyme—a strange succession
of Grave and Gay. Those here selected are strung
into something of an Eclogue, with perhaps a less
than equal proportion of the " Drink and make-
merry," which (genuine or not) recurs over-frequently
in the Original. Either way; the Result is sad
enough : saddest perhaps when most ostentatiously

merry : more apt to move Sorrow than Anger toward
the old Tentmaker, who, after vainly endeavouring
to unshackle his Steps from Destiny, and to catch
some authentic Glimpse of TO-MORROW, fell back
upon TO-DAY (which has outlasted so many To-
morrows !) as the only Ground he had got to stand
upon, however momentarily slipping from under his
Feet.

While the second Edition of this version of Omar
was preparing, Monsieur Nicolas, French Consul at
Resht, published a very careful and very good
Edition of the Text, from a lithograph copy at
Teheran, comprising 464 Rubáiyát, with translation
and notes of his own.

Mons. Nicolas, whose Edition has reminded me
of several things, and instructed me in others, does
not consider Omar to be the material Epicurean that
I have literally taken him for, but a Mystic, shadow-
ing the Deity under the figure of Wine, Wine-bearer.

etc., as Háfiz is supposed to do; in short, a Súfi Poet like Háfiz and the rest.

I cannot see reason to alter my opinion, formed as it was more than a dozen years ago [1] when Omar was first shown me by one to whom I am indebted for all I know of Oriental, and very much of other, literature. He admired Omar's Genius so much, that he would gladly have adopted any such Interpretation of his meaning as Mons. Nicolas' if he could. [2] That he could not, appears by his Paper in the *Calcutta Review* already so largely quoted; in which he argues from the Poems themselves, as well as from what records remain of the Poet's Life.

And if more were needed to disprove Mons. Nicolas' Theory, there is the Biographical Notice which he himself has drawn up in direct contra-

---

[1] [This was written in 1868.—W. A. W.]

[2] Perhaps would have edited the Poems himself some years ago. He may now as little approve of my Version on one side, as of Mons. Nicolas' Theory on the other.

diction to the Interpretation of the Poems given in his Notes. (See pp. xiii. xiv. of his Preface.) Indeed I hardly knew poor Omar was so far gone till his Apologist informed me. For here we see that, whatever were the Wine that Háfiz drank and sang, the veritable Juice of the Grape it was which Omar used, not only when carousing with his friends, but (says Mons. Nicolas) in order to excite himself to that pitch of Devotion which others reached by cries and "hurlemens." And yet, whenever Wine, Wine-bearer, etc., occur in the text—which is often enough—Mons. Nicolas carefully annotates "Dieu," "La Divinité," etc. : so carefully indeed that one is tempted to think that he was indoctrinated by the Súfi with whom he read the Poems. (Note to Rub. II. p. 8.) A Persian would naturally wish to vindicate a distinguished Countryman : and a Súfi to enrol him in his own sect, which already comprises all the chief poets in Persia.

What historical Authority has Mons. Nicolas to

show that Omar gave himself up "avec passion à l'étude de la philosophie des Soufis"? (Preface, p. xiii.) The Doctrines of Pantheism, Materialism, Necessity, etc., were not peculiar to the Súfi; nor to Lucretius before them; nor to Epicurus before him; probably the very original Irreligion of Thinking men from the first; and very likely to be the spontaneous growth of a Philosopher living in an Age of social and political barbarism, under shadow of one of the Two-and-Seventy Religions supposed to divide the world. Von Hammer (according to Sprenger's Oriental Catalogue) speaks of Omar as " a Free-thinker, and *a great opponent of Sufism;*" perhaps because, while holding much of their Doctrine, he would not pretend to any inconsistent severity of morals. Sir W. Ouseley has written a note to something of the same effect on the fly-leaf of the Bodleian MS. And in two Rubáiyát of Mons. Nicolas' own Edition Súf and Súfi are both disparagingly named.

No doubt many of these Quatrains seem unaccountable unless mystically interpreted; but many more as unaccountable unless literally. Were the Wine spiritual, for instance, how wash the Body with it when dead? Why make cups of the dead clay to be filled with —"La Divinité"—by some succeeding Mystic? Mons. Nicolas himself is puzzled by some "bizarres" and "trop Orientales" allusions and images—"d'une sensualité quelquefois révoltante" indeed—which "les convenances" do not permit him to translate; but still which the reader cannot but refer to "La Divinité."[1]   No doubt also many of the

[1] A Note to Quatrain 234 admits that, however clear the mystical meaning of such Images must be to Europeans, they are not quoted without "rougissant" even by laymen in Persia— "Quant aux termes de tendresse qui commencent ce quatrain, comme tant d'autres dans ce recueil, nos lecteurs, habitués maintenant à l'étrangeté des expressions si souvent employées par Khéyam pour rendre ses pensées sur l'amour divin, et à la singularité de ses images trop orientales, d'une sensualité quelquefois révoltante, n'auront pas de peine à se persuader qu'il s'agit de la Divinité, bien que cette conviction soit vivement discutée par les moullahs musulmans et même par

Quatrains in the Teheran, as in the Calcutta, Copies, are spurious ; such *Rubáiyát* being the common form of Epigram in Persia.   But this, at best, tells as much one way as another ; nay, the Súfi, who may be considered the Scholar and Man of Letters in Persia, would be far more likely than the careless Epicure to interpolate what favours his own view of the Poet.   I observe that very few of the more mystical Quatrains are in the Bodleian MS. which must be one of the oldest, as dated at Shiráz, A.H. 865, A.D. 1460.   And this, I think, especially dis tinguishes Omar (I cannot help calling him by his— no, not Christian—familiar name) from all other Persian Poets : That, whereas with them the Poet is lost in his Song, the Man in Allegory and Abstrac- tion ; we seem to have the Man—the *Bonhomme*— Omar himself, with all his Humours and Passions, as

beaucoup de laïques, qui rougissent véritablement d'une pareille licence de leur compatriote à l'égard des choses spirituelles."

frankly before us as if we were really at Table with
him, after the Wine had gone round.

I must say that I, for one, never wholly believed
in the Mysticism of Háfiz. It does not appear there
was any danger in holding and singing Súfi Pantheism, so long as the Poet made his Salaam to
Mohammed at the beginning and end of his Song.
Under such conditions Jeláluddín, Jámí, Attár, and
others sang; using Wine and Beauty indeed as
Images to illustrate, not as a Mask to hide, the
Divinity they were celebrating. Perhaps some Allegory less liable to mistake or abuse had been better
among so inflammable a People: much more so
when, as some think with Háfiz and Omar, the
abstract is not only likened to, but identified with,
the sensual Image; hazardous, if not to the Devotee
himself, yet to his weaker Brethren; and worse for
the Profane in proportion as the Devotion of the
Initiated grew warmer. And all for what? To be
tantalized with Images of sensual enjoyment which

must be renounced if one would approximate a God, who according to the Doctrine, *is* Sensual Matter as well as Spirit, and into whose Universe one expects unconsciously to merge after Death, without hope of any posthumous Beatitude in another world to compensate for all one's self-denial in this. Lucretius' blind Divinity certainly merited, and probably got, as much self-sacrifice as this of the Súfi ; and the burden of Omar's Song—if not " Let us eat "—is assuredly—" Let us drink, for To-morrow we die ! " And if Háfiz meant quite otherwise by a similar language, he surely miscalculated when he devoted his Life and Genius to so equivocal a Psalmody as, from his Day to this, has been said and sung by any rather than Spiritual Worshippers.

However, as there is some traditional presumption, and certainly the opinion of some learned men, in favour of Omar's being a Súfi—and even something of a Saint—those who please may so interpret his Wine and Cup-bearer. On the other hand, as there is far more historical certainty of his being a Philosopher, of scientific Insight and Ability far beyond that of the Age and Country he lived in ; of such moderate worldly Ambition as becomes a Philosopher, and such moderate wants as rarely satisfy a Debauchee ; other readers may be content to believe with me that, while the Wine Omar celebrates is simply the Juice of the Grape, he bragged more than he drank of it, in very defiance perhaps of that Spiritual Wine which left its Votaries sunk in Hypocrisy or Disgust.

RUBÁIYÁT

OF

OMAR KHAYYÁM OF NAISHÁPÚR

I

WAKE! For the Sun, who scatter'd into flight
The Stars before him from the Field of Night,
  Drives Night along with them from Heav'n, and
      strikes
The Sultán's Turret with a Shaft of Light.

II

Before the phantom of False morning died,
Methought a Voice within the Tavern cried,
  "When all the Temple is prepared within,
Why nods the drowsy Worshipper outside?"

III

And, as the Cock crew, those who stood before
The Tavern shouted—" Open then the Door !
    You know how little while we have to stay,
And, once departed, may return no more."

IV

Now the New Year reviving old Desires,
The thoughtful Soul to Solitude retires,
    Where the WHITE HAND OF MOSES on the Bough
Puts out, and Jesus from the Ground suspires.

V

Íram indeed is gone with all his Rose,
And Jamshýd's Sev'n-ring'd Cup where no one
       knows ;
    But still a Ruby kindles in the Vine,
And many a Garden by the Water blows.

VI

And David's lips are lockt; but in divine
High-piping Pehleví, with " Wine ! Wine ! Wine !
   Red Wine ! "—the Nightingale cries to the Rose
That sallow cheek of hers to incarnadine.

VII

Come, fill the Cup, and in the fire of Spring
Your Winter-garment of Repentance fling :
   The Bird of Time has but a little way
To flutter—and the Bird is on the Wing.

VIII

Whether at Naishápúr or Babylon,
Whether the Cup with sweet or bitter run,
   The Wine of Life keeps oozing drop by drop,
The Leaves of Life keep falling one by one.

IX

Each Morn a thousand Roses brings, you say;
Yes, but where leaves the Rose of Yesterday?
    And this first Summer month that brings the Rose
Shall take Jamshýd and Kaikobád away.

X

Well, let it take them! What have we to do
With Kaikobád the Great, or Kaikhosrú?
    Let Zál and Rustum bluster as they will,
Or Hátim call to Supper—heed not you.

XI

With me along the strip of Herbage strown
That just divides the desert from the sown,
    Where name of Slave and Sultán is forgot—
And Peace to Mahmúd on his golden Throne!

XII

A Book of Verses underneath the Bough,
A Jug of Wine, a Loaf of Bread—and Thou
   Beside me singing in the Wilderness—
Oh, Wilderness were Paradise enow!

XIII

Some for the Glories of This World; and some
Sigh for the Prophet's Paradise to come;
   Ah, take the Cash, and let the Credit go,
Nor heed the rumble of a distant Drum!

XIV

Look to the blowing Rose about us—"Lo,
Laughing," she says, "into the world I blow.
   At once the silken tassel of my Purse
Tear, and its Treasure on the Garden throw."

XV

And those who husbanded the Golden grain,
And those who flung it to the winds like Rain,
    Alike to no such aureate Earth are turn'd
As, buried once, Men want dug up again.

XVI

The Worldly Hope men set their Hearts upon
Turns Ashes—or it prospers; and anon,
    Like Snow upon the Desert's dusty Face,
Lighting a little hour or two—is gone.

XVII

Think, in this batter'd Caravanserai
Whose Portals are alternate Night and Day,
    How Sultán after Sultán with his Pomp
Abode his destined Hour, and went his way.

XVIII

They say the Lion and the Lizard keep
The Courts where Jamshýd gloried and drank deep :
   And Bahrám, that great Hunter—the Wild Ass
Stamps o'er his Head, but cannot break his Sleep.

XIX

I sometimes think that never blows so red
The Rose as where some buried Cæsar bled ;
   That every Hyacinth the Garden wears
Dropt in her Lap from some once lovely Head.

XX

And this reviving Herb whose tender Green
Fledges the River-Lip on which we lean—
   Ah, lean upon it lightly ! for who knows
From what once lovely Lip it springs unseen !

XXI

Ah, my Belovéd, fill the Cup that clears
TO-DAY of past Regrets and Future Fears:
    To-morrow!—Why, To-morrow I may be
Myself with Yesterday's Sev'n thousand Years.

XXII

For some we loved, the loveliest and the best
That from his Vintage rolling Time hath prest,
    Have drunk their Cup a Round or two before,
And one by one crept silently to rest.

XXIII

And we, that now make merry in the Room
They left, and Summer dresses in new bloom,
    Ourselves must we beneath the Couch of Earth
Descend—ourselves to make a Couch—for whom?

XXIV

Ah, make the most of what we yet may spend,
Before we too into the Dust descend;
  Dust into Dust, and under Dust to lie
Sans Wine, sans Song, sans Singer, and—sans End!

XXV

Alike for those who for TO-DAY prepare,
And those that after some TO-MORROW stare,
  A Muezzín from the Tower of Darkness cries,
"Fools! your Reward is neither Here nor There!"

XXVI

Why, all the Saints and Sages who discuss'd
Of the Two Worlds so wisely—they are thrust
  Like foolish Prophets forth; their Words to Scorn
Are scatter'd, and their Mouths are stopt with Dust.

XXVII

Myself when young did eagerly frequent
Doctor and Saint, and heard great argument
  About it and about : but evermore
Came out by the same door where in I went.

XXVIII

With them the seed of Wisdom did I sow,
And with mine own hand wrought to make it grow ;
  And this was all the Harvest that I reap'd—
" I came like Water, and like Wind I go."

XXIX

Into this Universe, and *Why* not knowing
Nor *Whence*, like Water willy-nilly flowing ;
  And out of it, as Wind along the Waste,
I know not *Whither*, willy-nilly blowing.

XXX

What, without asking, hither hurried *Whence?*
And, without asking, *Whither* hurried hence!
   Oh, many a Cup of this forbidden Wine
Must drown the memory of that insolence!

XXXI

Up from Earth's Centre through the Seventh Gate
I rose, and on the Throne of Saturn sate;
   And many a Knot unravel'd by the Road;
But not the Master-knot of Human Fate.

XXXII

There was the Door to which I found no Key:
There was the Veil through which I might not see:
   Some little talk awhile of ME and THEE
There was—and then no more of THEE and ME.

XXXIII

Earth could not answer; nor the Seas that mourn
In flowing Purple, of their Lord forlorn;
   Nor rolling Heaven, with all his Signs reveal'd
And hidden by the sleeve of Night and Morn.

XXXIV

Then of the THEE IN ME who works behind
The Veil, I lifted up my hands to find
   A Lamp amid the Darkness; and I heard,
As from Without—"THE ME WITHIN THEE BLIND!

XXXV

Then to the lip of this poor earthen Urn
I lean'd, the Secret of my Life to learn:
   And Lip to Lip it murmur'd—"While you live,
Drink!—for, once dead, you never shall return."

XXXVI

I think the Vessel, that with fugitive
Articulation answer'd, once did live,
   And drink ; and Ah ! the passive Lip I kiss'd,
How many Kisses might it take—and give !

XXXVII

For I remember stopping by the way
To watch a Potter thumping his wet Clay :
   And with its all-obliterated Tongue
It murmur'd—" Gently, Brother, gently, pray !"

XXXVIII

And has not such a Story from of Old
Down Man's successive generations roll'd
   Of such a clod of saturated Earth
Cast by the Maker into Human mould ?

XXXIX

And not a drop that from our Cups we throw
For Earth to drink of, but may steal below
   To quench the fire of Anguish in some Eye
There hidden—far beneath, and long ago.

XL

As then the Tulip for her morning sup
Of Heav'nly Vintage from the soil looks up,
   Do you devoutly do the like, till Heav'n
To Earth invert you—like an empty Cup.

XLI

Perplext no more with Human or Divine,
To-morrow's tangle to the winds resign,
   And lose your fingers in the tresses of
The Cypress-slender Minister of Wine.

XLII

And if the Wine you drink, the Lip you press,
End in what All begins and ends in—Yes ;
   Think then you are TO-DAY what YESTERDAY
You were—TO-MORROW you shall not be less.

XLIII

So when that Angel of the darker Drink
At last shall find you by the river-brink,
   And, offering his Cup, invite your Soul
Forth to your Lips to quaff—you shall not shrink.

XLIV

Why, if the Soul can fling the Dust aside,
And naked on the Air of Heaven ride,
   Were't not a Shame—were't not a Shame for him
In this clay carcase crippled to abide ?

D

XLV

'Tis but a Tent where takes his one day's rest
A Sultán to the realm of Death addrest ;
   The Sultán rises, and the dark Ferrásh
Strikes, and prepares it for another Guest.

XLVI

And fear not lest Existence closing your
Account, and mine, should know the like no more ;
   The Eternal Sákí from that Bowl has pour'd
Millions of Bubbles like us, and will pour.

XLVII

When You and I behind the Veil are past,
Oh, but the long, long while the World shall last,
   Which of our Coming and Departure heeds
As the Sea's self should heed a pebble-cast.

XLVIII

A Moment's Halt—a momentary taste
Of BEING from the Well amid the Waste—
   And Lo!—the phantom Caravan has reach'd
The NOTHING it set out from—Oh, make haste!

XLIX

Would you that spangle of Existence spend
About THE SECRET—quick about it, Friend!
   A Hair perhaps divides the False and True—
And upon what, prithee, may life depend?

L

A Hair perhaps divides the False and True;
Yes; and a single Alif were the clue—
   Could you but find it—to the Treasure-house,
And peradventure to THE MASTER too;

LI

Whose secret Presence, through Creation's veins
Running Quicksilver-like eludes your pains;
　　Taking all shapes from Máh to Máhi; and
They change and perish all—but He remains;

LII

A moment guess'd—then back behind the Fold
Immerst of Darkness round the Drama roll'd
　　Which, for the Pastime of Eternity,
He doth Himself contrive, enact, behold.

LIII

But if in vain, down on the stubborn floor
Of Earth, and up to Heav'n's unopening Door,
　　You gaze TO-DAY, while You are You—how then
TO-MORROW, You when shall be You no more?

LIV

Waste not your Hour, nor in the vain pursuit
Of This and That endeavour and dispute ;
   Better be jocund with the fruitful Grape
Than sadden after none, or bitter, Fruit.

LV

You know, my Friends, with what a brave Carouse
I made a Second Marriage in my house ;
   Divorced old barren Reason from my Bed,
And took the Daughter of the Vine to Spouse.

LVI

For "Is" and "Is-not" though with Rule and Line
And "Up-and-down" by Logic I define,
   Of all that one should care to fathom, I
Was never deep in anything but—Wine.

LVII

Ah, but my Computations, People say,

Reduced the Year to better reckoning?—Nay,

'Twas only striking from the Calendar

Unborn To-morrow, and dead Yesterday.

LVIII

And lately, by the Tavern Door agape,

Came shining through the Dusk an Angel Shape

Bearing a Vessel on his Shoulder; and

He bid me taste of it; and 'twas—the Grape!

LIX

The Grape that can with Logic absolute

The Two-and-Seventy jarring Sects confute:

The sovereign Alchemist that in a trice

Life's leaden metal into Gold transmute:

LX

The mighty Mahmúd, Allah-breathing Lord,
That all the misbelieving and black Horde
  Of Fears and Sorrows that infest the Soul
Scatters before him with his whirlwind Sword.

LXI

Why, be this Juice the growth of God, who dare
Blaspheme the twisted tendril as a Snare ?
  A Blessing, we should use it, should we not ?
And if a Curse—why, then, Who set it there ?

LXII

I must abjure the Balm of Life, I must,
Scared by some After-reckoning ta'en on trust,
  Or lured with Hope of some Diviner Drink,
To fill the Cup—when crumbled into Dust !

LXIII

Oh threats of Hell and Hopes of Paradise !
One thing at least is certain—*This* Life flies ;
　　One thing is certain and the rest is Lies ;
The Flower that once has blown for ever dies.

LXIV

Strange, is it not ? that of the myriads who
Before us pass'd the door of Darkness through,
　　Not one returns to tell us of the Road,
Which to discover we must travel too.

LXV

The Revelations of Devout and Learn'd
Who rose before us, and as Prophets burn'd,
　　Are all but Stories, which, awoke from Sleep
They told their comrades, and to Sleep return'd.

LXVI

I sent my Soul through the Invisible,
Some letter of that After-life to spell:
  And by and by my Soul return'd to me,
And answer'd "I Myself am Heav'n and Hell:"

LXVII

Heav'n but the Vision of fulfill'd Desire,
And Hell the Shadow from a Soul on fire,
  Cast on the Darkness into which Ourselves,
So late emerged from, shall so soon expire.

LXVIII

We are no other than a moving row
Of Magic Shadow-shapes that come and go
  Round with the Sun-illumined Lantern held
In Midnight by the Master of the Show;

LXIX

But helpless Pieces of the Game He plays
Upon this Chequer-board of Nights and Days ;
    Hither and thither moves, and checks, and slays,
And one by one back in the Closet lays.

LXX

The Ball no question makes of Ayes and Noes,
But Here or There as strikes the Player goes ;
    And He that toss'd you down into the Field,
He knows about it all—HE knows—HE knows !

LXXI

The Moving Finger writes ; and, having writ,
Moves on : nor all your Piety nor Wit
    Shall lure it back to cancel half a Line,
Nor all your Tears wash out a Word of it.

LXXII

And that inverted Bowl they call the Sky,

Whereunder crawling coop'd we live and die,

   Lift not your hands to *It* for help—for It

As impotently moves as you or I.

LXXIII

With Earth's first Clay They did the Last Man knead,

And there of the Last Harvest sow'd the Seed :

   And the first Morning of Creation wrote

What the Last Dawn of Reckoning shall read.

LXXIV

YESTERDAY *This* Day's Madness did prepare ;

TO-MORROW'S Silence, Triumph, or Despair :

   Drink ! for you know not whence you came, nor

      why :

Drink ! for you know not why you go, nor where.

LXXV

I tell you this—When, started from the Goal,
Over the flaming shoulders of the Foal
    Of Heav'n Parwín and Mushtarí they flung,
In my predestined Plot of Dust and Soul

LXXVI

The Vine had struck a fibre : which about
If clings my being—let the Dervish flout ;
    Of my Base metal may be filed a Key,
That shall unlock the Door he howls without.

LXXVII

And this I know : whether the one True Light
Kindle to Love, or Wrath-consume me quite,
    One Flash of It within the Tavern caught
Better than in the Temple lost outright.

LXXVIII

What ! out of senseless Nothing to provoke
A conscious Something to resent the yoke
   Of unpermitted Pleasure, under pain
Of Everlasting Penalties, if broke !

LXXIX

What ! from his helpless Creature be repaid
Pure Gold for what he lent him dross-allay'd—
   Sue for a Debt he never did contract,
And cannot answer—Oh the sorry trade !

LXXX

Oh Thou, who didst with pitfall and with gin
Beset the Road I was to wander in,
   Thou wilt not with Predestined Evil round
Enmesh, and then impute my Fall to Sin !

LXXXI

Oh, Thou, who Man of baser Earth didst make,
And ev'n with Paradise devise the Snake :
  For all the Sin wherewith the Face of Man
Is blacken'd—Man's forgiveness give—and take !

*   *   *   *

LXXXII

As under cover of departing Day
Slunk hunger-stricken Ramazán away,
  Once more within the Potter's house alone
I stood, surrounded by the Shapes of Clay.

LXXXIII

Shapes of all Sorts and Sizes, great and small,
That stood along the floor and by the wall ;
  And some loquacious Vessels were ; and some
Listen'd perhaps, but never talk'd at all.

LXXXIV

Said one among them—" Surely not in vain
My substance of the common Earth was ta'en
  And to this Figure moulded, to be broke,
Or trampled back to shapeless Earth again."

LXXXV

Then said a Second—" Ne'er a peevish Boy
Would break the Bowl from which he drank in joy ;
  And He that with his hand the Vessel made
Will surely not in after Wrath destroy."

LXXXVI

After a momentary silence spake
Some Vessel of a more ungainly Make ;
  " They sneer at me for leaning all awry :
What ! did the Hand then of the Potter shake ? "

LXXXVII

Whereat some one of the loquacious Lot—
I think a Súfi pipkin—waxing hot—
    "All this of Pot and Potter—Tell me then,
Who is the Potter, pray, and who the Pot?"

LXXXVIII

"Why," said another, "Some there are who tell
Of one who threatens he will toss to Hell
    The luckless Pots he marr'd in making—Pish!
He's a Good Fellow, and 't will all be well."

LXXXIX

"Well," murmur'd one, "Let whoso make or buy,
My Clay with long Oblivion is gone dry:
    But fill me with the old familiar Juice,
Methinks I might recover by and by."

XC

So while the Vessels one by one were speaking,
The little Moon look'd in that all were seeking:
    And then they jogg'd each other, "Brother! Brother!
Now for the Porter's shoulder-knot a-creaking!"

*   *   *   *

XCI

Ah, with the Grape my fading Life provide,
And wash the Body whence the Life has died,
    And lay me, shrouded in the living Leaf,
By some not unfrequented Garden-side.

XCII

That ev'n my buried Ashes such a snare
Of Vintage shall fling up into the Air
    As not a True-believer passing by
But shall be overtaken unaware.

E

XCIII

Indeed the Idols I have loved so long
Have done my credit in this World much wrong :
　　Have drown'd my Glory in a shallow Cup
And sold my Reputation for a Song.

XCIV

Indeed, indeed, Repentance oft before
I swore—but was I sober when I swore ?
　　And then and then came Spring, and Rose-in-hand
My thread-bare Penitence apieces tore.

XCV

And much as Wine has play'd the Infidel,
And robb'd me of my Robe of Honour—Well,
　　I wonder often what the Vintners buy
One half so precious as the stuff they sell.

XCVI

Yet Ah, that Spring should vanish with the Rose!
That Youth's sweet-scented manuscript should close!
  The Nightingale that in the branches sang,
Ah whence, and whither flown again, who knows!

XCVII

Would but the Desert of the Fountain yield
One glimpse—if dimly, yet indeed, reveal'd,
  To which the fainting Traveller might spring,
As springs the trampled herbage of the field!

XCVIII

Would but some wingéd Angel ere too late
Arrest the yet unfolded Roll of Fate,
  And make the stern Recorder otherwise
Enregister, or quite obliterate!

XCIX

Ah Love! could you and I with Him conspire
To grasp this sorry Scheme of Things entire,
   Would not we shatter it to bits—and then
Re-mould it nearer to the Heart's Desire!

      *   *   *   *

C

Yon rising Moon that looks for us again—
How oft hereafter will she wax and wane;
   How oft hereafter rising look for us
Through this same Garden—and for *one* in vain!

CI

And when like her, oh Sákí, you shall pass
Among the Guests Star-scatter'd on the Grass,
   And in your joyous errand reach the spot
Where I made One—turn down an empty Glass!

TAMÁM

NOTES

(Stanza II.) The "*False Dawn*"; *Subhi Kázib*, a transient Light on the Horizon about an hour before the *Subhi sádik*, or True Dawn; a well-known Phenomenon in the East.

(IV.) New Year. Beginning with the Vernal Equinox, it must be remembered; and (howsoever the old Solar Year is practically superseded by the clumsy *Lunar* Year that dates from the Mohammedan Hijra) still commemorated by a Festival that is said to have been appointed by the very Jamshýd whom Omar so often talks of, and whose yearly Calendar he helped to rectify.

"The sudden approach and rapid advance of the Spring," says Mr. Binning,[1] "are very striking. Before the Snow is well off the Ground, the Trees burst into Blossom, and the Flowers start forth from the Soil. At *Now Rooz* [*their* New Year's Day] the Snow was lying in patches on the Hills and in the shaded Vallies, while the Fruit-trees in the Gardens were budding beautifully, and green Plants and Flowers springing up on the Plains on every side—

> 'And on old Hyems' Chin and icy Crown
> An odorous Chaplet of sweet Summer buds
> Is, as in mockery, set.'—

[1] *Two Years' Travel in Persia*, etc., i. 165.

Among the Plants newly appeared I recognised some old
Acquaintances I had not seen for many a Year : among these,
two varieties of the Thistle—a coarse species of Daisy like
the ' Horse - gowan ' — red and white Clover — the Dock —
the blue Corn-flower — and that vulgar Herb the Dandelion
rearing its yellow crest on the Banks of the Water-courses."
The Nightingale was not yet heard, for the Rose was not
yet blown ; but an almost identical Blackbird and Wood-
pecker helped to make up something of a North - country
Spring.

"The White Hand of Moses."   Exodus iv. 6 ; where
Moses draws forth his Hand—not, according to the Persians,
" *leprous as Snow*,"—but *white*, as our May-blossom in Spring
perhaps.   According to them also the Healing Power of Jesus
resided in His Breath.

(v.) Iram, planted by King Shaddád, and now sunk some-
where in the Sands of Arabia.   Jamshýd's Seven-ring'd Cup
was typical of the 7 Heavens, 7 Planets, 7 Seas, etc., and was
a *Divining Cup*.

(vi.) *Pehleví*, the old Heroic *Sanskrit* of Persia.   Háfiz
also speaks of the Nightingale's *Pehleví*, which did not change
with the People's.

I am not sure if the fourth line refers to the Red Rose
looking sickly, or to the Yellow Rose that ought to be Red ;
Red, White, and Yellow Roses all common in Persia.   I think
that Southey, in his Common-Place Book, quotes from some
Spanish author about the Rose being White till 10 o'clock ;
" Rosa Perfecta " at 2 ; and " perfecta incarnada " at 5.

(x.) Rustum, the " Hercules " of Persia, and Zál his Father, whose exploits are among the most celebrated in the Sháh-náma. Hátim Tai, a well-known type of Oriental Generosity.

(XIII.) A Drum—beaten outside a Palace.

(XIV.) That is, the Rose's Golden Centre.

(XVIII.) Persepolis: call'd also *Takht-i-Jamshýd*—THE THRONE OF JAMSHÝD, "*King Splendid,*" of the mythical *Peshdádian* Dynasty, and supposed (according to the Sháh-náma) to have been founded and built by him. Others refer it to the Work of the Genie King, Ján Ibn Ján—who also built the Pyramids—before the time of Adam.

BAHRÁM GÚR—*Bahrám of the Wild Ass*—a Sassanian Sovereign—had also his Seven Castles (like the King of Bohemia!) each of a different Colour: each with a Royal Mistress within; each of whom tells him a Story, as told in one of the most famous Poems of Persia, written by Amír Khusraw: all these Seven also figuring (according to Eastern Mysticism) the Seven Heavens; and perhaps the Book itself that Eighth, into which the mystical Seven transcend, and within which they revolve. The Ruins of Three of those Towers are yet shown by the Peasantry; as also the swamp in which Bahrám sunk, like the Master of Ravenswood, while pursuing his *Gúr*.

The Palace that to Heav'n his pillars threw,
And Kings the forehead on his threshold drew—
    I saw the solitary Ringdove there,
And "Coo, coo, coo," she cried; and "Coo, coo, coo."

This Quatrain Mr. Binning found, among several of Háfiz and others, inscribed by some stray hand among the ruins of

Persepolis.   The Ringdove's ancient *Pehleví Coo, Coo, Coo*, signifies also in Persian " *Where? Where? Where?* "   In Attár's " Bird-parliament " she is reproved by the Leader of the Birds for sitting still, and for ever harping on that one note of lamentation for her lost Yúsuf.

Apropos of Omar's Red Roses in Stanza xix., I am reminded of an old English superstition, that our Anemone Pulsatilla, or purple " Pasque Flower " (which grows plentifully about the Fleam Dyke, near Cambridge), grows only where Danish blood has been spilt.

(XXI.) A thousand years to each Planet.

(XXXI.) Saturn, Lord of the Seventh Heaven.

(XXXII.) ME-AND-THEE : some dividual Existence or Personality distinct from the Whole.

(XXXVII.) One of the Persian Poets—Attár, I think—has a pretty story about this.   A thirsty Traveller dips his hand into a Spring of Water to drink from.   By and by comes another who draws up and drinks from an earthen Bowl, and then departs, leaving his Bowl behind him.   The first Traveller takes it up for another draught ; but is surprised to find that the same Water which had tasted sweet from his own hand tastes bitter from the earthen Bowl.   But a Voice—from Heaven, I think—tells him the clay from which the Bowl is made was once *Man ;* and, into whatever shape renewed, can never lose the bitter flavour of Mortality.

(XXXIX.) The custom of throwing a little Wine on the ground before drinking still continues in Persia, and perhaps generally in the East.   Mons. Nicolas considers it " un signe de libéralité, et en même temps un avertissement que le buveur doit vider sa coupe jusqu'à la dernière goutte." Is it not more likely an ancient Superstition ; a Libation to propitiate Earth, or make her an Accomplice in the illicit Revel? Or, perhaps, to divert the Jealous Eye by some sacrifice of superfluity, as with the Ancients of the West? With Omar we see something more is signified ; the precious Liquor is not lost, but sinks into the ground to refresh the dust of some poor Wine-worshipper foregone.

Thus Háfiz, copying Omar in so many ways : "When thou drinkest Wine pour a draught on the ground. Wherefore fear the Sin which brings to another Gain?"

(XLIII.) According to one beautiful Oriental Legend, Azräel accomplishes his mission by holding to the nostril an Apple from the Tree of Life.

This and the two following Stanzas would have been withdrawn, as somewhat *de trop*, from the Text, but for advice which I least like to disregard.

(LI.) From Máh to Máhi ; from Fish to Moon.

(LVI.) A Jest, of course, at his Studies. A curious mathematical Quatrain of Omar's has been pointed out to me ; the more curious because almost exactly parallel'd by some Verses of Doctor Donne's, that are quoted in Izaak Walton's Lives ! Here is Omar : "You and I are the image of a pair of compasses ; though we have two heads (sc. our *feet*) we have one body ; when we have fixed the centre for our circle, we bring our heads (sc. feet) together at the end." Dr. Donne :

> If we be two, we two are so
> As stiff twin-compasses are two ;

Thy Soul, the fixt foot, makes no show
　　To move, but does if the other do.

And though thine in the centre sit,
　　Yet when my other far does roam,
Thine leans and hearkens after it,
　　And grows erect as mine comes home.

Such thou must be to me, who must
　　Like the other foot obliquely run ;
Thy firmness makes my circle just,
　　And me to end where I begun.

(LIX.) The Seventy-two Religions supposed to divide the World, *including* Islamism, as some think : but others not.

(LX.) Alluding to Sultan Mahmúd's Conquest of India and its dark people.

(LXVIII.) *Fánúsi khiyál*, a Magic-lantern still used in India ; the cylindrical Interior being painted with various Figures, and so lightly poised and ventilated as to revolve round the lighted Candle within.

(LXX.) A very mysterious Line in the Original :

O dánad O dánad O dánad O——

breaking off something like our Wood-pigeon's Note, which she is said to take up just where she left off.

(LXXV.) Parwín and Mushtarí—The Pleiads and Jupiter.

(LXXXVII.) This Relation of Pot and Potter to Man and his Maker figures far and wide in the Literature of the World, from the time of the Hebrew Prophets to the present ; when it may finally take the name of " Pot theism," by which Mr. Carlyle ridiculed Sterling's "Pantheism." *My* Sheikh, whose knowledge flows in from all quarters, writes to me—

"Apropos of old Omar's Pots, did I ever tell ycu the sentence I found in Bishop Pearson on the Creed? ' Thus are we wholly at the disposal of His will, and our present and future condition framed and ordered by His free, but wise and just, decrees. *Hath not the potter power over the clay, of the same lump to make one vessel unto honour, and another unto dishonour?* (Rom. ix. 21.) And can that earth-artificer have a freer power over his *brother potsherd* (both being made of the same metal), than God hath over him, who, by the strange fecundity of His omnipotent power, first made the clay out of nothing, and then him out of that?' "

And again—from a very different quarter—" I had to refer the other day to Aristophanes, and came by chance on a curious Speaking-pot story in the *Vespæ*, which I had quite forgotten.

Φιλοκλέων.　"Ακουε, μὴ φεῦγ'· ἐν Συβάρει γυνή ποτε l. 1435
　　　　　　κατέαξ' ἐχῖνον.

Κατήγορος.　　　　　　　Ταῦτ' ἐγὼ μαρτύρομαι.

Φι.　　　Οὐχῖνος οὖν ἔχων τιν' ἐπεμαρτύρατο·
　　　　Εἶθ' ἡ Συβαρῖτις εἶπεν, εἰ ναὶ τὰν κόραν
　　　　τὴν μαρτυρίαν ταύτην ἐάσας, ἐν τάχει
　　　　ἐπίδεσμον ἐπρίω, νοῦν ἂν εἶχες πλείονα.

"The Pot calls a bystander to be a witness to his bad treatment. The woman says, 'If, by Proserpine, instead of all this "testifying" (comp. Cuddie and his mother in *Old Mortality!*) you would buy yourself a rivet, it would show more

sense in you !'   The Scholiast explains *echinus* as ἄγγος τι ἐκ
κεράμου."

One more illustration for the oddity's sake from the
Autobiography of a Cornish Rector, by the late James
Hamley Tregenna.   1871.

"There was one old Fellow in our Company—he was so
like a Figure in the *Pilgrim's Progress* that Richard always
called him the 'ALLEGORY,' with a long white beard—a rare
Appendage in those days—and a Face the colour of which
seemed to have been baked in, like the Faces one used to see
on Earthenware Jugs.   In our Country-dialect Earthenware is
called ' *Clome* '; so the Boys of the Village used to shout out
after him—' Go back to the Potter, old Clome-face, and get
baked over again.'   For the 'Allegory,' though shrewd enough in
most things, had the reputation of being *saift-baked, i.e.* of
weak intellect."

(XC.) At the Close of the Fasting Month, Ramazán (which
makes the Mussulman unhealthy and unamiable), the first
Glimpse of the New Moon (who rules their division of the Year)
is looked for with the utmost Anxiety, and hailed with
Acclamation.   Then it is that the Porter's Knot may be
heard—toward the *Cellar*.   Omar has elsewhere a pretty
Quatrain about the same Moon—

>   " Be of Good Cheer—the sullen Month will die,
>   And a young Moon requite us by and by :
>   Look how the Old one, meagre, bent, and wan
>   With Age and Fast, is fainting from the Sky ! "

[*The first Edition of the translation of Omar Khayyám, which appeared in 1859, differs so much from those which followed, that it has been thought better to print it in full, instead of attempting to record the differences.*]

I

Awake! for Morning in the Bowl of Night
Has flung the Stone that puts the Stars to Flight:
    And Lo! the Hunter of the East has caught
The Sultán's Turret in a Noose of Light.

II

Dreaming when Dawn's Left Hand was in the Sky
I heard a Voice within the Tavern cry,
    "Awake, my Little ones, and fill the Cup
Before Life's Liquor in its Cup be dry."

III

And, as the Cock crew, those who stood before
The Tavern shouted—" Open then the Door!

    You know how little while we have to stay,
And, once departed, may return no more."

IV

Now the New Year reviving old Desires,
The thoughtful Soul to Solitude retires,

    Where the WHITE HAND OF MOSES on the Bough
Puts out, and Jesus from the Ground suspires.

V

Irám indeed is gone with all its Rose,
And Jamshýd's Sev'n-ring'd Cup where no one
        knows;

    But still the Vine her ancient Ruby yields,
And still a Garden by the Water blows.

VI

And David's Lips are lock't ; but in divine
High piping Pehleví, with " Wine ! Wine ! Wine !
   Red Wine ! "—the Nightingale cries to the Rose
That yellow Cheek of her's to incarnadine.

VII

Come, fill the Cup, and in the Fire of Spring
The Winter Garment of Repentance fling :
   The Bird of Time has but a little way
To fly—and Lo ! the Bird is on the Wing.

VIII

And look—a thousand Blossoms with the Day
Woke—and a thousand scatter'd into Clay :
   And this first Summer Month that brings the Rose
Shall take Jamshýd and Kaikobád away

IX

But come with old Khayyám, and leave the Lot
Of Kaikobád and Kaikhosrú forgot :
  Let Rustum lay about him as he will,
Or Hátim Tai cry Supper—heed them not.

X

With me along some Strip of Herbage strown
That just divides the desert from the sown,
  Where name of Slave and Sultán scarce is known,
And pity Sultán Máhmúd on his Throne.

XI

Here with a Loaf of Bread beneath the Bough,
A Flask of Wine, a Book of Verse—and Thou
  Beside me singing in the Wilderness—
And Wilderness is Paradise enow.

XII

" How sweet is mortal Sovranty !"—think some :
Others—" How blest the Paradise to come ! "
    Ah, take the Cash in hand and waive the Rest ;
Oh, the brave Music of a *distant* Drum !

XIII

Look to the Rose that blows about us—" Lo,
Laughing, " she says, " into the World I blow :
    At once the silken Tassel of my Purse
Tear, and its Treasure on the Garden throw. "

XIV

The Worldly Hope men set their Hearts upon
Turns Ashes—or it prospers ; and anon,
    Like Snow upon the Desert's dusty Face
Lighting a little Hour or two—is gone.

F

XV

And those who husbanded the Golden Grain,
And those who flung it to the Winds like Rain,
    Alike to no such aureate Earth are turn'd
As, buried once, Men want dug up again.

XVI

Think, in this batter'd Caravanserai
Whose Doorways are alternate Night and Day,
    How Sultán after Sultán with his Pomp
Abode his Hour or two, and went his way.

XVII

They say the Lion and the Lizard keep
The Courts where Jamshýd gloried and drank deep;
    And Bahrám, that great Hunter—the Wild Ass
Stamps o'er his Head, and he lies fast asleep.

XVIII

I sometimes think that never blows so red
The Rose as where some buried Cæsar bled ;
  That every Hyacinth the Garden wears
Dropt in its Lap from some once lovely Head.

XIX

And this delightful Herb whose tender Green
Fledges the River's Lip on which we lean—
  Ah, lean upon it lightly ! for who knows
From what once lovely Lip it springs unseen !

XX

Ah, my Belovéd, fill the Cup that clears
TO-DAY of past Regrets and future Fears—
  To-morrow ?—Why, To-morrow I may be
Myself with Yesterday's Sev'n Thousand Years.

XXI

Lo ! some we loved, the loveliest and best
That Time and Fate of all their Vintage prest,
    Have drunk their Cup a Round or two before,
And one by one crept silently to Rest.

XXII

And we, that now make merry in the Room
They left, and Summer dresses in new Bloom,
    Ourselves must we beneath the Couch of Earth
Descend, ourselves to make a Couch—for whom ?

XXIII

Ah, make the most of what we yet may spend,
Before we too into the Dust descend ;
    Dust into Dust, and under Dust, to lie,
Sans Wine, sans Song, sans Singer, and—sans End !

XXIV

Alike for those who for TO-DAY prepare,
And those that after a TO-MORROW stare,
  A Muezzín from the Tower of Darkness cries
"Fools! your Reward is neither Here nor There!"

XXV

Why, all the Saints and Sages who discuss'd
Of the Two Worlds so learnedly, are thrust
  Like foolish Prophets forth; their Words to Scorn
Are scatter'd, and their Mouths are stopt with Dust.

XXVI

Oh, come with old Khayyám, and leave the Wise
To talk; one thing is certain, that Life flies;
  One thing is certain, and the Rest is Lies;
The Flower that once has blown for ever dies.

XXVII

Myself when young did eagerly frequent
Doctor and Saint, and heard great Argument
   About it and about : but evermore
Came out by the same Door as in I went.

XXVIII

With them the Seed of Wisdom did I sow,
And with my own hand labour'd it to grow :
   And this was all the Harvest that I reap'd—
" I came like Water, and like Wind I go."

XXIX

Into this Universe, and *why* not knowing,
Nor *whence*, like Water willy-nilly flowing :
   And out of it, as Wind along the Waste,
I know not *whither*, willy-nilly blowing.

XXX

What, without asking, hither hurried *whence ?*
And, without asking, *whither* hurried hence !
  Another and another Cup to drown
The Memory of this Impertinence !

XXXI

Up from Earth's Centre through the Seventh Gate
I rose, and on the Throne of Saturn sate,
  And many Knots unravel'd by the Road ;
But not the Knot of Human Death and Fate.

XXXII

There was a Door to which I found no Key :
There was a Veil past which I could not see :
  Some little Talk awhile of ME and THEE
There seem'd—and then no more of THEE and ME.

XXXIII

Then to the rolling Heav'n itself I cried,
Asking, " What Lamp had Destiny to guide
    Her little Children stumbling in the Dark ? "
And—" A blind Understanding ! " Heav'n replied.

XXXIV

Then to this earthen Bowl did I adjourn
My Lip the secret Well of Life to learn :
    And Lip to Lip it murmur'd—" While you live
Drink !—for once dead you never shall return. "

XXXV

I think the Vessel, that with fugitive
Articulation answer'd, once did live,
    And merry-make ; and the cold Lip I kiss'd
How many Kisses might it take—and give !

XXXVI

For in the Market-place, one Dusk of Day,
I watch'd the Potter thumping his wet Clay:
 And with its all obliterated Tongue
It murmur'd—"Gently, Brother, gently, pray!"

XXXVII

Ah, fill the Cup:—what boots it to repeat
How Time is slipping underneath our Feet:
 Unborn TO-MORROW, and dead YESTERDAY,
Why fret about them if TO-DAY be sweet!

XXXVIII

One Moment in Annihilation's Waste,
One Moment, of the Well of Life to taste—
 The Stars are setting and the Caravan
Starts for the Dawn of Nothing—Oh, make haste!

XXXIX

How long, how long, in infinite Pursuit
Of This and That endeavour and dispute?
   Better be merry with the fruitful Grape
Than sadden after none, or bitter, Fruit.

XL

You know, my Friends, how long since in my House
For a new Marriage I did make Carouse:
   Divorced old barren Reason from my Bed,
And took the Daughter of the Vine to Spouse.

XLI

For "Is" and "Is-not" though *with* Rule and Line
And "Up-and-down" *without*, I could define,
   I yet in all I only cared to know,
Was never deep in anything but—Wine.

XLII

And lately, by the Tavern Door agape,
Came stealing through the Dusk an Angel Shape
   Bearing a Vessel on his Shoulder ; and
He bid me taste of it ; and 'twas—the Grape !

XLIII

The Grape that can with Logic absolute
The Two-and-Seventy jarring Sects confute :
   The subtle Alchemist that in a Trice
Life's leaden Metal into Gold transmute.

XLIV

The mighty Mahmúd, the victorious Lord,
That all the misbelieving and black Horde
   Of Fears and Sorrows that infest the Soul
Scatters and slays with his enchanted Sword.

XLV

But leave the Wise to wrangle, and with me
The Quarrel of the Universe let be :
    And, in some corner of the Hubbub coucht,
Make Game of that which makes as much of Thee.

XLVI

For in and out, above, about, below,
'Tis nothing but a Magic Shadow-show,
    Play'd in a Box whose Candle is the Sun,
Round which we Phantom Figures come and go.

XLVII

And if the Wine you drink, the Lip you press,
End in the Nothing all Things end in—Yes—
    Then fancy while Thou art, Thou art but what
Thou shalt be—Nothing—Thou shalt not be less.

XLVIII

While the Rose blows along the River Brink,
With old Khayyám the Ruby Vintage drink :
  And when the Angel with his darker Draught
Draws up to Thee—take that, and do not shrink.

XLIX

'Tis all a Chequer-board of Nights and Days
Where Destiny with Men for Pieces plays :
  Hither and thither moves, and mates, and slays,
And one by one back in the Closet lays.

L

The Ball no Question makes of Ayes and Noes,
But Right or Left as strikes the Player goes ;
  And He that toss'd Thee down into the Field,
He knows about it all—HE knows—HE knows !

LI

The Moving Finger writes; and, having writ,
Moves on : nor all thy Piety nor Wit
    Shall lure it back to cancel half a Line,
Nor all thy Tears wash out a Word of it.

´ LII

And that inverted Bowl we call The Sky,
Whereunder crawling coop't we live and die,
    Lift not thy hands to *It* for help—for It
Rolls impotently on as Thou or I.

LIII

With Earth's first Clay They did the Last Man's
        knead,
And then of the Last Harvest sow'd the Seed :
    Yea, the first Morning of Creation wrote
What the Last Dawn of Reckoning shall read.

LIV

I tell Thee this—When, starting from the Goal,
Over the shoulders of the flaming Foal
   Of Heav'n Parwín and Mushtara they flung,
In my predestined Plot of Dust and Soul

LV

The Vine had struck a Fibre ; which about
If clings my Being—let the Súfi flout ;
   Of my Base Metal may be filed a Key,
That shall unlock the Door he howls without,

LVI

And this I know : whether the one True Light,
Kindle to Love, or Wrath consume me quite,
   One glimpse of It within the Tavern caught
Better than in the Temple lost outright.

LVII

Oh Thou, who didst with Pitfall and with Gin
Beset the Road I was to wander in,
  Thou wilt not with Predestination round
Enmesh me, and impute my Fall to Sin?

LVIII

Oh, Thou, who Man of baser Earth didst make,
And who with Eden didst devise the Snake;
  For all the Sin wherewith the Face of Man
Is blacken'd, Man's Forgiveness give—and take!

*   *   *   *

KÚZA-NÁMA

LIX

Listen again.   One evening at the Close
Of Ramazán, ere the better Moon arose,
  In that old Potter's Shop I stood alone
With the clay Population round in Rows.

LX

And, strange to tell, among that Earthen Lot
Some could articulate, while others not :
  And suddenly one more impatient cried—
"Who *is* the Potter, pray, and who the Pot ?"

LXI

Then said another—" Surely not in vain
My Substance from the common Earth was ta'en,
  That He who subtly wrought me into Shape
Should stamp me back to common Earth again."

G

LXII

Another said—"Why, ne'er a peevish Boy,
Would break the Bowl from which he drank in Joy;
    Shall He that *made* the Vessel in pure Love
And Fancy, in an after Rage destroy!"

LXIII

None answer'd this; but after Silence spake
A Vessel of a more ungainly Make:
    "They sneer at me for leaning all awry;
What! did the Hand then of the Potter shake?

LXIV

Said one—"Folks of a surly Tapster tell,
And daub his Visage with the Smoke of Hell;
    They talk of some strict Testing of us—Pish!
He's a Good Fellow, and 'twill all be well."

LXV

Then said another with a long-drawn Sigh,
" My Clay with long oblivion is gone dry :
    But, fill me with the old familiar Juice,
Methinks I might recover by-and-bye ! "

LXVI

So while the Vessels one by one were speaking,
One spied the little Crescent all were seeking :
    And then they jogg'd each other, " Brother !
        Brother !
Hark to the Porter's Shoulder-knot a creaking ! "

*   *   *   *

LXVII

Ah, with the Grape my fading Life provide,
And wash my Body whence the Life has died,
    And in a Windingsheet of Vine-leaf wrapt,
So bury me by some sweet Garden-side.

LXVIII

That ev'n my buried Ashes such a Snare
Of Perfume shall fling up into the Air,

As not a True Believer passing by
But shall be overtaken unaware.

LXIX

Indeed the Idols I have loved so long
Have done my Credit in Men's Eye much wrong :

Have drown'd my Honour in a shallow Cup,
And sold my Reputation for a Song.

LXX

Indeed, indeed, Repentance oft before
I swore—but was I sober when I swore ?

And then and then came Spring, and Rose-in-hand
My thread-bare Penitence apieces tore.

LXXI

And much as Wine has play'd the Infidel,
And robb'd me of my Robe of Honour—well,
   I often wonder what the Vintners buy
One half so precious as the Goods they sell.

LXXII

Alas, that Spring should vanish with the Rose!
That Youth's sweet-scented Manuscript should close!
   The Nightingale that in the Branches sang,
Ah, whence, and whither flown again, who knows!

LXXIII

Ah Love! could thou and I with Fate conspire
To grasp this sorry Scheme of Things entire,
   Would not we shatter it to bits—and then
Re-mould it nearer to the Heart's Desire!

LXXIV

Ah, Moon of my Delight who know'st no wane,
The Moon of Heav'n is rising once again :
　　How oft hereafter rising shall she look
Through this same Garden after me—in vain !

LXXV

And when Thyself with shining Foot shall pass
Among the Guests Star-scatter'd on the Grass,
　　And in thy joyous Errand reach the Spot
Where I made one—turn down an empty Glass !

TAMÁM SHUD

VARIATIONS

BETWEEN THE SECOND, THIRD AND FOURTH EDITIONS OF

OMAR KHAYYÁM

STANZA

I.   In ed. 2 :

> Wake ! For the Sun behind yon Eastern height
> Has chased the Session of the Stars from Night ;
>   And, to the field of Heav'n ascending, strikes
> The Sultán's Turret with a Shaft of Light.

In the first draught of ed. 3 the first and second lines stood thus :

> Wake ! For the Sun before him into Night
> A Signal flung that put the Stars to flight.

II.   In ed. 2 :

> Why lags the drowsy Worshipper outside ?

V.   In edd. 2 and 3 :

> But still a Ruby gushes from the Vine.

IX.   In ed. 2 :

> Morning a thousand Roses brings, you say.

X.   In ed. 2 :

> Let Rustum cry "To Battle !" as he likes,
> Or Hátim Tai "To Supper !"—heed not you.

STANZA

X.   In ed. 3 :

        Let Zál and Rustum thunder as they will.

XII.   In ed. 2 :

        Here with a little Bread beneath the Bough,
        A Flask of Wine, a Book of Verse—and Thou etc.

XIII.   In ed. 2 :

           Ah, take the Cash, and let the Promise go,
        Nor heed the music of a distant Drum !

XV.   In the first line, ed. 2 and the first draught of
        ed. 3 have '' For those, etc.''

XVI.   In line 4, edd. 2 and 3 read '' was gone.''

XX.   In ed. 2 :

        And this delightful Herb whose living Green
        Fledges the River's Lip on which we lean.

XXI.   In edd. 2 and 3, '' past Regret.''

XXII.   In edd. 2 and 3 :

        That from his Vintage rolling Time has prest.

XXVI.   In edd. 2 and 3 :

        Of the Two Worlds so learnedly, are thrust.

XXVII.   In ed. 2 :

        Came out by the same door as in I went.

XXVIII.   In edd. 2 and 3 :

        And with my own hand wrought to make it grow.

XXX.   In ed. 2 :

           Ah, contrite Heav'n endowed us with the Vine
        To drug the memory of that insolence !

STANZA

XXXI.   In ed. 2 :

    And many Knots unravel'd by the Road.

XXXII.   In edd. 2 and 3 :

    There was the Veil through which I could not see.

XXXIII.   In ed. 2 :

    Nor Heaven, with those eternal Signs reveal'd.

XXXIV.   In ed. 2 :

    Then of the THEE IN ME who works behind
    The Veil of Universe I cried to find
        A Lamp to guide me through the darkness ; and
    Something then said—" An Understanding blind."

XXXV.   In ed. 2 :

    I lean'd, the secret Well of Life to learn.

XXXVI.   In ed. 2 :

    And drink ; and that impassive Lip I kiss'd.

XXXVIII. In ed. 2 the only difference is " For " instead of
        " And " in the first line ; but in the first draught
        of ed. 3 the stanza appeared thus :

    For, in your Ear a moment— of the same
    Poor Earth from which that Human Whisper came,
        The luckless Mould in which Mankind was cast
    They did compose, and call'd him by the name.

    In ed. 3 the first line was altered to—

    Listen—a moment listen !—Of the same etc.

XXXIX.   In ed. 2 :

    On the parcht herbage but may steal below.

STANZA

XL. In ed. 2 :

As then the Tulip for her wonted sup
Of Heavenly Vintage lifts her chalice up,
   Do you, twin offspring of the soil, till Heav'n
To Earth invert you like an empty Cup.

In the first draught of ed. 3 the stanza is the same as
   in edd. 3 and 4, except that the second line is—
Of Wine from Heav'n her little Tass lifts up.

XLI. In ed. 2 and the first draught of ed. 3 :

Oh, plagued no more with Human or Divine,
To-morrow's tangle to itself resign.

XLII. In ed. 2 :

And if the Cup you drink, the Lip you press,
End in what All begins and ends in—Yes ;
   Imagine then you *are* what heretofore
You *were*—hereafter you shall not be less.

The first draught of ed. 3 agrees with edd. 3 and 4
   except that the first line is—
And if the Cup, and if the Lip you press.

XLIII. In ed. 2 :

So when at last the Angel of the drink
Of Darkness finds you by the river-brink,
   And, proffering his Cup, invites your Soul
Forth to your Lips to quaff it—do not shrink.

In the first draught of ed. 3 the only change made was
   from " proffering " to " offering," but in ed. 3

STANZA

> the stanza assumed the form in which it also appeared in ed. 4. The change from " the Angel " to " that Angel " was made in MS. by FitzGerald in a copy of ed. 4.

XLIV.   In ed. 2 :

> Is't not a shame—is't not a shame for him
> So long in this Clay suburb to abide !

XLV.   In ed. 2 :

> But that is but a Tent wherein may rest.

XLVI.   In ed. 2 :

> And fear not lest Existence closing *your*
> Account, should lose, or know the type no more.

XLVII.   In ed. 2 :

> As much as Ocean of a pebble-cast.

In ed. 3 :

> As the SEV'N SEAS should heed a pebble-cast.

XLVIII.   In ed. 2 :

> One Moment in Annihilation's Waste,
> One Moment, of the Well of Life to taste—
> The Stars are setting, and the Caravan
> Draws to the Dawn of Nothing — Oh make haste.

In the first draught of ed. 3 the third line originally stood :

> Before the starting Caravan has reach'd

the rest of the stanza being as in edd. 3 and 4.

STANZA

XLIX.   In ed. 2 :

        A Hair, they say, divides the False and True.
        The change from "does" to "may" in the last line
           was made by FitzGerald in MS.

L.   In ed. 2 :

        A Hair, they say, divides the False and True.

LII.   In ed. 2 and 3 :

        He does Himself contrive, enact, behold.

LIII.   In the first draught of ed. 3 :

        To-morrow, when You shall be You no more.

LIV.   In ed. 2 :

        Better be merry with the fruitful Grape.

LV.   In ed. 2 :

        You know, my Friends, how bravely in my House
        For a new Marriage I did make Carouse.

LVII.   In ed. 2 :

        Have squared the Year to Human Compass, eh ?
          If so, by striking from the Calendar.

LXII.   In ed. 2 :

        When the frail Cup is crumbled into Dust !

LXIII.   In ed. 2 :

        The Flower that once is blown for ever dies.

LXV.   In edd. 2 and 3

        They told their fellows, and to Sleep return'd.

STANZA

LXVI.   In ed. 2 :

      And after many days my Soul return'd

      And said, " Behold, Myself am Heav'n and Hell."

LXVII.   In edd. 2 and 3 :

      And Hell the Shadow of a Soul on fire.

LXVIII. In ed. 2 :

      Of visionary Shapes that come and go

      Round with this Sun-illumin'd Lantern held.

    Ed. 3 also retains " this."

LXIX.   In edd. 2 and 3 :

      Impotent Pieces of the Game He plays.

LXX.   In edd. 2 and 3 :

      But Right or Left as strikes the Player goes.

LXXI.   In ed. 3, " Piety and Wit."

LXXII.   In ed. 2 and the first draught of ed. 3 :

      And that inverted Bowl we call The Sky.

    In edd. 2 and 3 :

      As impotently rolls as you or I.

LXXIX.   In edd. 2 and 3 :

      Pure Gold for what he lent us dross-allay'd.

LXXXI.   In ed. 2 :

      For all the Sin the Face of wretched Man

      Is black with—Man's Forgiveness give—and take !

LXXXIII. In ed. 2 :

      And once again there gather'd a scarce heard

      Whisper among them ; as it were, the stirr'd

      Ashes of some all but extinguisht Tongue

      Which mine ear kindled into living Word.

STANZA

LXXXIV. In ed. 2 :

My Substance from the common Earth was ta'en,
That He who subtly wrought me into Shape
Should stamp me back to shapeless Earth again ?

LXXXV. In ed. 2 :

Another said—" Why, ne'er a peevish Boy
Would break the Cup from which he drank in Joy ;
Shall He that of His own free Fancy made
The Vessel, in an after-rage destroy ! "

LXXXVI. In ed. 2 :

None answer'd this ; but after silence spake.

LXXXVII. In ed. 2 :

Thus with the Dead as with the Living, *What ?*
And *Why ?* so ready, but the *Wherefor* not,
One on a sudden peevishly exclaim'd,
" Which is the Potter, pray, and which the Pot ? "

In ed. 3 the last line reads :

Who makes—Who sells—Who buys—Who *is* the
Pot ?

LXXXVIII. In ed. 2 :

Said one—" Folks of a surly Master tell,
And daub his Visage with the Smoke of Hell ,
They talk of some sharp Trial of us—Pish !
He's a Good Fellow, and 'twill all be well."

In the first draught of ed. 3 the stanza begins :

" Why," said another, " Dismal people tell
Of an old Savage who will toss to Hell
The luckless Pots, etc."

LXXXIX. In ed. 2 :

" Well," said another, " Whoso will, let try:

STANZA

XC. In ed. 2 :

 One spied the little Crescent all were seeking.

XCI. In ed. 2 :

 And wash my Body whence the Life has died.

XCIII. In ed. 2 :

 Have done my credit in Men's eye much wrong.

XCV. In ed. 2 :

 I often wonder what the Vintners buy
 One half so precious as the ware they sell.

XCVII. In ed. 2 :

 Toward which the fainting Traveller might spring.

XCVIII. In ed. 2 :

 Oh if the World were but to re-create,

 That we might catch ere closed the Book of Fate,

 And make The Writer on a fairer leaf

 Inscribe our names, or quite obliterate !

XCIX. In ed. 2 :

 Ah Love ! could you and I with Fate conspire.

C. In ed. 2 :

 But see ! The rising Moon of Heav'n again

 Looks for us, Sweet-heart, through the quivering
  Plane :

 How oft hereafter rising will she look

 Among those leaves—for one of us in vain !

CI. In ed. 2 :

 And when Yourself with silver Foot shall pass.

 In the first draught of ed. 3 " Foot " is changed to
  " step."

 In ed. 3 :

 And in your blissful errand reach the spot.

STANZAS WHICH APPEAR IN THE SECOND EDITION ONLY

XIV.   Were it not Folly, Spider-like to spin
         The Thread of present Life away to win—
            What? for ourselves, who know not if we shall
         Breathe out the very Breath we now breathe in!

XX.   (This stanza is quoted in the note to stanza XVIII. in
         the third and fourth editions.)

XXVIII.   Another Voice, when I am sleeping, cries,
         "The Flower should open with the Morning skies."
            And a retreating Whisper, as I wake—
         "The Flower that once has blown for ever dies.'

XLIV.   Do you, within your little hour of Grace,
         The waving Cypress in your Arms enlace,
            Before the Mother back into her arms
         Fold, and dissolve you in a last embrace.

LXV.   If but the Vine and Love-abjuring Band
         Are in the Prophet's Paradise to stand,
            Alack, I doubt the Prophet's Paradise
         Were empty as the hollow of one's Hand.

LXXVII.   For let Philosopher and Doctor preach
        Of what they will, and what they will not—each
           Is but one Link in an eternal Chain
        That none can slip, nor break, nor over-reach.

LXXXVI.   Nay, but, for terror of his wrathful Face,
        I swear I will not call Injustice Grace,
           Not one Good Fellow of the Tavern but
        Would kick so poor a Coward from the place.

XC.   And once again there gather'd a scarce heard
        Whisper among them ; as it were, the stirr'd
           Ashes of some all but extinguisht Tongue,
        Which mine ear kindled into living Word.

(In the third and fourth editions stanza LXXXIII. takes the place
    of this.)

XCIX.   Whither resorting from the vernal Heat
        Shall Old Acquaintance Old Acquaintance greet,
           Under the Branch that leans above the Wall
        To shed his Blossom over head and feet.

(This was retained in the first draught of ed. 3.)

CVII.   Better, oh better, cancel from the Scroll
        Of Universe one luckless Human Soul,
           Than drop by drop enlarge the Flood that rolls
        Hoarser with Anguish as the Ages Roll.

COMPARATIVE TABLE OF STANZAS IN
THE FOUR EDITIONS

Ed. 1	Ed. 2	Edd. 3 and 4
I	I	I
II	II	II
III	III	III
IV	IV	IV
V	V	V
VI	VI	VI
VII	VII	VII
VIII	IX	IX
IX	X	X
X	XI	XI
XI	XII	XII
XII	XIII	XIII
XIII	XV	XIV
XIV	XVII	XVI
XV	XVI	XV
XVI	XVIII	XVII
XVII	XIX	XVIII
XVIII	XXIV	XIX
XIX	XXV	XX

Ed. 1	Ed. 2	Edd. 3 and 4
XX	XXI	XXI
XXI	XXII	XXII
XXII	XXIII	XXIII
XXIII	XXVI	XXIV
XXIV	XXVII	XXV
XXV	XXIX	XXVI
XXVI	LXVI	LXIII
XXVII	XXX	XXVII
XXVIII	XXXI	XXVIII
XXIX	XXXII	XXIX
XXX	XXXIII	XXX
XXXI	XXXIV	XXXI
XXXII	XXXV	XXXII
XXXIII	XXXVII	XXXIV
XXXIV	XXXVIII	XXXV
XXXV	XXXIX	XXXVI
XXXVI	XL	XXXVII
XXXVII		
XXXVIII	XLIX	XLVIII
XXXIX	LVI	LIV
XL	LVII	LV
XLI	LVIII	LVI
XLII	LX	LVIII
XLIII	LXI	LIX
XLIV	LXII	LX
XLV		
XLVI	LXXIII	LXVIII

Ed. 1	Ed. 2	Edd. 3 and 4
XLVII	XLV	XLII
XLVIII	XLVI	XLIII
XLIX	LXXIV	LXIX
L	LXXV	LXX
LI	LXXVI	LXXI
LII	LXXVIII	LXXII
LIII	LXXIX	LXXIII
LIV	LXXXI	LXXV
LV	LXXXII	LXXVI
LVI	LXXXIII	LXXVII
LVII	LXXXVII	LXXX
LVIII	LXXXVIII	LXXXI
LIX	LXXXIX	LXXXII
LX	XCIV	LXXXVII
LXI	XCI	LXXXIV
LXII	XCII	LXXXV
LXIII	XCIII	LXXXVI
LXIV	XCV	LXXXVIII
LXV	XCVI	LXXXIX
LXVI	XCVII	XC
LXVII	XCVIII	XCI
LXVIII	C	XCII
LXIX	CI	XCIII
LXX	CII	XCIV
LXXI	CIII	XCV
LXXII	CIV	XCVI
LXXIII	CVIII	XCIX

Ed. 1	Ed. 2	Edd. 3 and 4
LXXIV	CIX	C
LXXV	CX	CI
	VIII	VIII
	XIV	
Note on		Note on
XVII	XX	XVIII
	XXVIII	
	XXXVI	XXXIII
	XLI	XXXVIII
	XLII	XXXIX
	XLIII	XL
	XLIV	
	XLVII	XLVI
	XLVIII	XLVII
	L	XLIX
	LI	L
	LII	LI
	LIII	LII
	LIV	LIII
	LV	XLI
	LIX	LVII
	LXIII	LXI
	LXIV	LXII
	LXV	
	LXVII	LXIV
	LXVIII	LXV

Ed. 1	Ed. 2	Edd. 3 and 4
Preface	LXIX	XLIV
do.	LXX	XLV
	LXXI	LXVI
	LXXII	LXVII
	LXXVII	
	LXXX	LXXIV
	LXXXIV	LXXVIII
	LXXXV	LXXIX
	LXXXVI	
	XC	LXXXIII
	XCIX	
	CV	XCVII
	CVI	XCVIII
	CVII	

NOTE BY THE EDITOR

It must be admitted that FitzGerald took great liberties with the original in his version of Omar Khayyám. The first stanza is entirely his own, and in stanza XXXIII. of the fourth edition (XXXVI. in the second) he has introduced two lines from Attár (See Letters, i. 320). In Stanza LXXXI. (fourth edition), writes Professor Cowell, "There is no original for the line about the snake : I have looked for it in vain in Nicolas ; but I have always supposed that the last line is FitzGerald's mistaken version of Quatr. 236 in Nicolas's ed. which runs thus :

" O thou who knowest the secrets of every one's mind,
  Who graspest every one's hand in the hour of weakness,
  O God, give me repentance and accept my excuses,
  O thou who givest repentance and acceptest the excuses of
      every one.

"FitzGerald mistook the meaning of *giving* and *accepting* as used here, and so invented his last line out of his own mistake. I wrote to him about it when I was in Calcutta ; but he never cared to alter it."

W. A. W.

THE END

PRINTED BY R. & R. CLARK, LTD., EDINBURGH